BLUE TANGO

also by Michael Van Walleghen
The Wichita Poems
More Trouble with the Obvious

POEMS BY
Michael Van Walleghen

BLUE TANGO

UNIVERSITY OF ILLINOIS PRESS
Urbana and Chicago

Publication of this work was supported in part by a grant
from the Illinois Arts Council, a state agency.

These poems first appeared in the following magazines:
The Iowa Review: "The Foot"; "Hanging On like Death";
    "The Age of Reason"; "Meat"
Ploughshares: "The Bottom Line"
The Southern Review: "Blue Tango"; "Roberta and
    Wilbur"
Ascent: "What's Wrong with UFO's?" (The first part of
    "What's Wrong with UFO's?" was initially published
    as "UFO's" in *Hub Bub.*)
The Hudson Review: "The Afterlife"; "Peach Isle"; "Who's
    There?"; "Starship Lands in Cornfield!"
Another Chicago Magazine: "Hidden Meaning"; "The
    Spoiled Child"
Columbia: "Bowling Alley"; "Worry"
Boulevard: "Tranquil Acres"
Midwest Review: "Sneaky"; "Atlantis"; "The Cat's
    Meow"; "Mother Bear, Father Bear"

"Lake Limbo" has been published in a broadside by John
    Koontz/Cumberland Books—Chax Press.

I wish to thank the National Endowment for the Arts,
the Illinois Arts Council, and the Center for Advanced
Study at the University of Illinois for their generous
support during the writing of this book.

Library of Congress Cataloging-in-Publication Data

Van Walleghen, Michael, 1938–
    Blue tango.

    I. Title.
PS3572.A545B5   1989   811'.54   88-17394
ISBN 0-252-06044-X (alk. paper)

for Pamela, Emily Lynn,
and my parents,
Joseph and Bernice

CONTENTS

1

THE FOOT

I rang his doorbell
every day for a month

I knocked on his windows
I kicked hard at his door

with my frozen Redwing boot.
It was winter of course

A month of deep snow. And
I could see from his slurred

footprints that he was home.
He was in there all right

reading the paper, watching
the tube maybe—the bastard.

He owed me five dollars.
Christmas was coming up.

And I was twelve years old
an ordinary paper boy

freezing my ass off, trying
to collect, that's all. Then

the door opens. A hot
sour wind, like cabbage

boiled in piss, springs up
from deep inside somewhere

and almost knocks me down.
"Here, you want it?" a voice

is saying. "Here, take it!"
And a shower of quarters

nickels, dimes goes sailing
past me over the porch rail.

When I look back, the door
is closed again, or rather

almost closed. A dirty foot
I remember his dirty foot

poking out into the snow
the filthy yellow thickness

of the toenails, the dead
gray, socklike grime

that covered it . . . I never saw
his face. I was too young

even to imagine it. I just
dug up the money I could

and ran home to the stoic
misery of my own dumb feet

thawing in a yellow dishpan.
Small, snow-white, delicate

they hurt for a long time
and looked all wrong somehow.

My face looked wrong . . . staring
back from the kitchen window

where it was night already
and the night looked wrong

as if there might be nothing
out there, that owed me anything.

WORRY

It was getting late
it was time for supper

but we had this rat
trapped in an oil drum

hydrophobic perhaps
and there was a hole

in the drum. Someone
had better do something

drop a brake drum on it
or better yet, perfect

if we could ever lift it
one of those fossil-looking

prewar transmissions
we'd spotted in the weeds . . .

On the other hand, suppose
we missed the goddamn thing

suppose we only crippled it?
We'd have to burn it then

or maybe we could drown it
if we plugged the hole somehow

if we had a hose or something
if even now the streetlights

might cease their flickering
and night not fall not fall

upon that fussy, worried knot
of small, good children there

in the twittering field
where the nightmare rats

were not afraid of anything
and swarmed and swarmed.

BOWLING ALLEY

There were six lanes
and a bar next door.

We worked two lanes
at a time. "Jumping"

it was called. Two
maybe three leagues

a night @ 13¢ a line
plus tips. It added up.

It was even kind of fun—
like being on a ship

and dodging broadsides
from the enemy. *Look*

lively lads! Right on.
You had to pay attention.

Otherwise a freak ricochet
could knock your teeth out.

And it was hot back there
concussive, sweat-slippery

a place I'd dream about
for years—an atmosphere

whistling with bombs
as I remember it

grapeshot, cannonballs
all the furious shrapnel

transposed and manifest
of beleaguered adolescence . . .

No wonder we got tired.
There was so much smoke

by the end of the night
we could hardly breathe—

we needed air back there
stars in the open hatchway

an icy, offshore gale
crashing on the gun deck . . .

until BANG we were done
the last pin racked

and we found ourselves
taking a leak in fact

out beside the Dumpster
in the literal alley

where it sometimes snowed.
One of us, I remember

had a tattoo. One of us
was missing some teeth.

HOLD IT

Hold it son, my boss would say
hold it right where you are

then came this little lecture
on correct procedure, advice

on how to hold a paintbrush
or mop the flooded restroom.

This was only my first job
so I had plenty to learn . . .

How to hold a screwdriver
for instance. Exactly right

precisely so. Lightbulbs
weren't so simple either

and sharpening a pencil
was practically impossible.

And yet, despite this close
tedious attention to detail

The Better Letter Service
the only thing he loved

was doomed. Julie, his wife
was an alcoholic for one thing

and for another, the telephones
had all been disconnected . . .

The trade in wedding invitations
invoices, flashy letterheads

evaporated overnight. Pigeons
disremembered flocks of them

were suddenly clamorous all day
under the tattered awnings . . .

Until it just seemed shiftless
not to poison them somehow.

We could burn their bodies
in the trash. Exactly right

precisely so. Our costumes
I remember, entailed goggles

rakes, appropriate brooms—
everything you might expect

by way of promoting correct
total incineration. The dead

however, kept showing up one
by one all winter. The dead

and the almost dead, the ones
who limped around in circles

or fluttered in the icy gutter.
The ones we had to strangle.

Hold it son, my boss would say
hold it right where you are

because a properly wrung neck
was pure technique after all

and the lighting of the pyre
a veritable art. Pushbrooms

matches, everything I touched
bristled with such complexity

I couldn't dream of quitting—
I could barely tie my shoe

and the shock of Julie's breasts
brushing loose along my arm

confused me utterly. *C'mon*
she'd whisper, *don't take things*

so serious. And then a hug.
But what, exactly, did it mean?

Ambiguous and undulant snow
a powdery, wraithlike mist

sifted down from the gutters
and glittered in the faltering

neon remnant of our sign . . .
Or perhaps another pigeon

limped around in circles
on the sidewalk. Nothing

but this by way of instruction
and nothing for overtime.

HIDDEN MEANING

Someone has parked her car
as far back as you can go

in Kickapoo Park—and now
she sits there eating candy

and listening to the radio . . .
A blinding, late November light

glitters on the windblown river.
A flurry of green cellophane

flutters from a side vent. Violins
banjos, that thin country voice

getting lost among the trees . . .
It all appears arranged somehow

charged with hidden meaning . . .
But what is it? Faint dogs

dim gunshots when the music stops . . .
Even the petty, disconsolate detail

of a coathanger bent into an aerial
becomes important—as in this light

the merest inkling of the moon
becomes a puff of frozen breath

or vague, translucent sail
stranded in the empty trees . . .

As in this light I might see myself
home on leave again from the navy

because my girl got pregnant
and we've come here to talk . . .

But later on, I'll meet my buddies
in the parking lot. Their cars

have names painted on them: *Virgo's
Good Time Machine, Evil Rasputin*

and the one called simply
Paranoia.

2

PEACH ISLE

First the sky turns green, then
green-black, crepitating, alive

with lightning. Car lights
start coming on, streetlights

the lights in riverside apartments—
while on the river there begins

a cacophony of anxious whistles
thunder, the clangorous alarms

of a channel buoy, close by . . .
This is not a good idea Joe

I hear my mother say. Already
an icy spray has soaked us

to the bone. Our stupid oars
are useless. We bobble merely

in the wake of motorboats, yachts—
everyone fleeing for cover but us

and the keening ore-boat dreadnoughts
anchored in the gloom above Peach Isle

our Sunday paradise and picnic spot.
I'm six weeks old on this picnic

an infant Jonah, fitfully asleep
still dreaming the panicky instant

of his own conception—dreaming
monstrous fish, the destruction

of cities, all the Hieronymus
Bosch landscapes of 1938 . . .

Let's throw him overboard Bernice
my father whispers. Otherwise

it starts to rain—egg-sized hail
starts bouncing from the seats

and we huddle there like refugees
machine-gunned in their dinghy . . .

Sinking instantly, sucked down
like the swatted flies I'd throw

years later, when the war was over
to sunfish on our bright lagoon—

eight years old, mysteriously alive
a stormy prince living with impostors.

MEAT

It was early Saturday, dawn
the day for buying meat . . .

My father had this friend
way over in Hamtramck

who knew all about meat
and so we'd drive uxorious

drunk mornings after payday
halfway across Detroit

to meet this expert
at the slaughterhouse

where they sold everything:
brains, testicles, tripe

all that precious offal
grocery stores disdained—

whole hog heads for headcheese
fresh duck blood, fresh feet

kidneys, giblets, pancreas . . .
The freshest meat in the world

my father's friend would shout
above the squealing, bleating

foaming panic of the animals
and my father would repeat it

all day long. *The freshest*
goddamn meat in the world

he'd croon to the barmaids
along our long route home

forgetting, even as he said it
that all that lovely meat

was spoiling in the car.
But I remembered. I knew

the trouble we were in.
I could already see us

opening the bloody packages—
our poor brains, our testicles

smelling up the whole kitchen
again, and in the sorry face

of all my father's promises
to come home early, sober

a fine example for his son
a good husband for a change

one of those smart guys
who knew all about meat.

THE AGE OF REASON

Once, my father got invited
by an almost perfect stranger

a four hundred pound alcoholic
who bought the drinks all day

to go really flying sometime
sightseeing in his Piper Cub

and my father said *Perfect!*
Tomorrow was my birthday

I'd be seven years old, a chip
off the old daredevil himself

and we'd love to go flying.
We'd even bring a case of beer.

My father weighed two fifty
two seventy-five in those days

the beer weighed something
the ice, the cooler. I weighed

practically nothing: forty-five
maybe fifty pounds at the most—

just enough to make me nervous.
Where were the parachutes? Who

was this guy? Then suddenly
there we were, lumbering

23

down a bumpy, too short runway
and headed for a fence . . .

Holy Shit! my father shouts
and that's it, all we need

by way of the miraculous
to lift us in a twinkling

over everything—fence, trees
and powerline. What a birthday!

We were really flying now . . .
We were probably high enough

to have another beer in fact,
high enough to see Belle Isle

the Waterworks, Packard's
and the Chrysler plant.

We could even see our own
bug-sized house down there

our own backyard, smaller
than a chewed-down thumbnail.

We wondered if my mother
was taking down the laundry

and if she'd wave . . . Lightning
trembled in the thunderheads

above Belle Isle. Altitude:
2,500; air speed: one twenty

but the fuel gauge I noticed
quivered right on empty . . .

I'd reached the age of reason.
Our pilot lit a big cigar.

THE CAT'S MEOW

At first he was going
to be a priest. Then

the depression hit
and he had to work.

Finally he found a job
working a punch press

at Briggs — a "butcher shop"
where doing piecework

meant missing fingers
hands mangled into claws . . .

But it's just about here
the story starts to wander.

At this point, my father
might talk about the guys

he hung around with, thugs
with names like "Killer George"

or "Two-Belly Buffalo Joe."
Other times he'd ramble on

about St. Edward's, assisting
the old monsignor at mass

and acting in that play
where he met my mother.

She was "the cat's meow"
as my father liked to say.

But then she got pregnant—
a detail I had to figure out

years later, all by myself.
Other details went nowhere—

dreamlike divagations
through old dance halls

corny pranks, stale jokes
from fifty years ago . . .

And then, as if by accident
he'd find himself once more

drinking in that crummy joint
adjacent to the factory . . .

A huge tomcat paced up
and down along the bar

one eye, mangled ears . . .
just the kind of mascot

you'd expect. Except
he needed to be fixed.

Anyone, even my father
could see that. And now

comes the strange part
the five-dollar bet

and my father shoving it
headfirst into an old boot

and just doing it, snicker
snack, with a pocketknife.

It all happens so fast
no one can believe it

not even my father
who pauses at this point

like a man discovering
his own flat fingers

splayed out in the die
of the uplifted press . . .

He can't figure it out.
It might even be funny

and so he laughs, ha-ha
like the old monsignor

when the innocent wine
began looking like blood.

THE SPOILED CHILD

The spoiled child
sits quiet as a mouse

and learns to deserve
everything he gets.

It's Christmas Eve

so naturally his father
kicks the electric train

tracks, station, cars and all
across the living room . . .

Next, he'll wrestle the goddamn
sonofabitch Christmas tree
right out of the house.

And furthermore, furthermore
if there's any more crying
any more talking back

the spoiled child
is going to get it again
with the strap.

*

The spoiled child
is exhausted by all this

and lies down in his bed
like a dog. His sleep
is full of yips and moans

but he's not a dog. Not
at all. There's simply
been an accident of sorts

a train wreck it turns out—
wreckage scattered everywhere

shouts, the breaking of glass . . .

then the nightlong, high-pitched
whistling of the broken boiler

the cruel, absolute zero
of deep space, live steam
condensing into stars

galaxies, the permanent
blizzard of the universe.

*

Just before true dawn

still bright, still there
at this chill latitude

the star of Bethlehem
sits low on the horizon

appearing as a tiny moon
or some far light leaking

from a bedroom keyhole . . .

God has placed it there
beyond all accident
the spoiled child thinks

and beyond all accident
he hears the Herald Angels
singing each to each . . .

They sound like bitter wind
the cold labyrinth of home
creaking in the wind, dogs

the knocking of pipes
the ragged, high-pitched
snoring of the Magi

the fitful shepherds
even the drunken Minotaur

uncomfortable on the couch
in his human body.

MOTHER BEAR, FATHER BEAR

"When the mother bear came after me
I ran to get my clothes and went back
outside the cage. But Juan started teas-
ing it and throwing bottles and sticks.
Then the father bear grabbed Juan by
the shoulder and dragged him toward
the cave."

—Sammy Farraj, age 10
UPI wireservice item

Deep in their black cave
beyond the iridescent moat
mother bear and father bear
were fast asleep. Elsewhere

twigs snap, birds wake up
and in the ape house something
screams like a little baby . . .
But the half-ton father bear

the heavy, worn-out mother
hear nothing at all. Who knows
what they were dreaming? Frozen
blood perhaps. Thalassic ice.

Some paradise of drifting snow
wherein they range omnipotent
free, and perfectly themselves . . .
Otherwise, their hot apartment

stinks like a backed-up sewer
and the moon is so much garbage
adrift again among the paper cups
and peanut shells. Otherwise

they wake up like monsters
in some poor child's nightmare:
beserk and ordinary parents
fighting over the half-eaten baby.

3

HANGING ON LIKE DEATH

The Octopus? The Tilt-a-Whirl?
Whatever it is, it begins

in the twinkling of an eye
to look like so much junk—

but it's too late by then.
By then, the jumpy alcoholic

who collects our tickets
has also strapped us in.

You'd have to be a little kid
to trust this thing. Tools

sinister, odd scraps of metal
scattered in the oily grass . . .

this ride looks absolutely
murderous. "Hang on now"

I tell my daughter. "Hang on."
What else is there to say

when the Octopus has got you?
Or suddenly, some cold, gray morning

a lavender Chevrolet Impala
with different colored doors

jumps the twisted guardrail
and then comes sliding toward you

sideways, down the interstate.
You'd have to be four years old

and afraid so far of nothing
in this life but monsters

big dogs and snakes to trust
this hanging on, this tilting world

about to vanish, this carnival
we almost missed—and *would* have

except for sheer dumb luck
and the kid who pumped our gas

and answered all our questions
by pointing here and there

along the flickering horizon
with a lit cigarette.

TRANQUIL ACRES

The tattered barn, farm junk
these star-infested trees . . .

I remember this. Moths
are fluttering everywhere

and limestone milky water
floods the little graveyard

just inside the gate. The barn
of course is full of monsters:

bulls, chained at the fetlock
chained at the nose. Of course.

Because that way, if he wanted to
a kid could take a walk in there

with nothing but his flashlight.
I remember this—the flashlight

sputtering like a wet match
lit up practically nothing at all

the merest tip of a horn perhaps
or maybe an eye, moth-white

plunging like a comet
through the clangorous dark . . .

Outside, it had begun to thunder
lightning trembled at the window

and then one of them tore loose
and jumped half out of his stall

screaming, his ripped-back nose
curled up like an elephant's trunk . . .

But all that happened years ago.
Of course, of course. Childhood

Child, is that you in there?
Did this really happen? Now

there's nothing here but moonlight
to remember you, nothing but moths

and the Milky Way together
swarming in the dendritic thicket

of the ruined orchard. Now
your innocence, pain and terror

recollected by this tranquil light
seem hardly childhood at all.

LAKE LIMBO

A cold drizzle
nearly every day
this week. The lake
green-gray, white-capped
the tiny beach littered
with oily dull debris
a wrack of styrofoam
weeds and plastic rope
and where the water stops
a yellowish stiff froth
shivers and flies apart
all morning all day
in the steady gale . . .

Even the snot-beaked
seagulls look marooned
and stand blearily around
in little gangs, freezing

flat broke, unemployed . . .

*

Behind the scenes somewhere
a kid with a black eye
a figment of the weather
starts chopping down a tree.

He's been on vacation now
since 1948. His parents
are probably next door
playing cards, drinking gin . . .

41

Listening to the lake
I can hear the slap slap
of his dull ax murdering
every tree in Michigan.

I can hear him muttering
like a lost motorboat.
I can hear him snarling
like a troubled chain saw.

Self-loathing, rage
childhood without end . . .
these are calibrations
on an old barometer

in love with the abysmal.
The air is full of ghosts
voices, an ironic yodeling
as from the same two loons

that shamed me as a boy
chopping idly at trees
or killing birds up here
with my BB gun. Everything

seems precisely as it was:
childhood at its very worst—
a Tierra del Fuego of desire
on the brink of paradise.

FISHING WITH CHILDREN

Beyond the few clear stumps
and furry sticks, the bottom
drops off quickly, quickly . . .

But it's easy enough to guess
the broken glass and junk
down there, the lost shoes

the stolen bike. Easier
to imagine trash like this
in the gray municipal lagoon

than fish in fact. The four
and five year olds however
keep seeing Northern Pike—

monster catfish. Even
the worms excite them.
What acrobats they are

especially cut in half!
Urged to bait their own hooks
they stand around staring

at the life in their hands
like so many self-involved
dumbstruck fortune-tellers.

Then they stab themselves
or tangle in the bushes . . .
the whole chaotic business

looking faintly Dionysian—
a manic kind of dance almost
or magic stone-age ritual

demanding blood. But later
cast out upon the dark water
our fateful bobbers drift

as over the face of the void
like stars. So we study them
of course, astrologers now

hoping for the smallest sign
or signal of good fortune—
a bluegill, anything at all

from that deep dead calm
where stars and even children
disappear. None of them

for the moment disappearing
though some look tremulous
and on the brink . . .

SNEAKY

Someone doesn't like cats—
he thinks they're "sneaky"

so cats start disappearing
all over the neighborhood.

Even our own cat disappears
and then, some weeks later

her mutilated body turns up
in an abandoned farmhouse—

because that's what she gets.
Someone doesn't like cats

so he stabs their eyes out
and cuts them into pieces.

Maniacs behind every tree.
Maniacs, child molesters . . .

But Emily, my five-year-old
has different notions entirely.

She thinks her cat's in Florida
on vacation—because it's winter

and "that's where the birds go."
It's winter, it's after supper

and a small moon, a cat's eye
follows us down our dark street

all the way to the liquor store—
then dimly, dimly back again . . .

Nevertheless, because she's eaten
so many raw carrots lately

my daughter informs me
she can see in the dark now

like the animals—whereupon
she leaps unerringly, catlike

over an ice-filled gutter—
at which, even the trees

seem stirred, clattering
their sudden applause

all round us for a moment—
then falling still as trees

near a house without windows
in the middle of winter.

THE BIG ANIMAL

It was probably a dog, but after wasting a whole day looking at vacation property, I thought our bored-to-tears four-year-old deserved whatever small excitements a decent father might invent—so I told her the tracks we'd found on the beach that afternoon at Whitefish Lake belonged to a wolverine or a small bear. Then we could pretend to be trailing it to see where it lived. We guessed rather obviously, as we puttered along, about why the tracks wandered here and there into the lake (he was thirsty, he needed a bath), but when they abruptly disappeared at the water's edge forever, I couldn't think of anything more to say. My daughter, on the other hand, thought he must have smelled something good to eat and probably just swam across the lake to someone's cottage to investigate. Perhaps he even looked in at the window and watched the people eat their supper.

"That's their place over there," my wife said finally, handing me the binoculars. She hadn't been listening. She meant the people the lady in the post office had told us about that morning. It seems the woman had fallen ill last spring sometime and now the husband needed cash in a hurry. It was lovely property—a narrow, rock-bound peninsula that pointed west across the lake to where we were. They had a little trailer on it but hadn't yet begun to build. I remember thinking how desperate someone would have to be to want to sell a place like that, and thinking too that it might be the bargain of a lifetime. Then I noticed the man, and what I took to be a nine- or ten-year-old girl, down by the water, climbing around on the rocks.

They looked like they'd just been swimming, but this was mid-October already. The water must have been freezing. All the cottages on their side of the lake looked empty. Even the trees were starting to look empty, despite their spotty brilliance, and the wooden docks were all pulled in and upside down beside the trailer, so they weren't there fishing. Had they come up all the way from Chicago then, in the middle of a school week, just to swim? My wife thought we should probably go over there and ask him if indeed the place was up for sale. Otherwise, we'd have to wait for a notice in the paper. I could see the girl shivering through the binoculars, a skinny blond with her hands held up to her mouth as if she wanted to shout something. Then her father wrapped her in a big towel and hugged her for a long time.

Anyway, it was getting late. Our four-year-old was starving for her supper . . . so tomorrow after all seemed good enough. We were staying in a little cabin back in the woods across the road from the lake, a flimsy tourist kind of place we'd rented for part of my sabbatical. Already, the nights were getting down to freezing. And that night in particular our daughter kept waking up terrified, her blankets scattered on the floor. She could hear that hungry wolverine she said, walking all around our cabin. He came from the other side of the lake but he wore clothes like a real person: a hat, a long scarf . . . "What do you think he likes to eat," I yawned, tired of this conversation, tired and cold and impatient for my bed. "He likes anything that people like because he thinks he's a person. But mostly," she said, "he likes leftovers—things in the garbage, and he eats children sometimes." An ordinary nightmare, in other words, an anxiety calmed by kisses, a firm, close tucking of the covers.

But the next morning, the people across the lake were gone. They must have left the previous evening or before dawn sometime, in the middle of the night. Nothing ever appeared in the paper about the property being for sale, but I still think of them, even now, years later. When they come to mind, the blond girl is always shouting something across the water, and I've also had a dream from time to time that begins with the girl and her father sitting down to supper. There's an old-fashioned lantern on the table and neither of them is speaking. Then the girl gets up and goes to the little window in the trailer door, as if she hears something. There's a complicated aluminum shutter on the window, the kind indigenous to trailers and tourist cabins, but after awhile the girl manages to get it open. And then I start shouting because a huge animal of some kind has his face to the window and stares and stares at the empty place.

4

SKATING ON THE BLACK LAGOON

After supper, after dark
they'd sneak out to the streetcar
then transfer to the screaming bus
that took them over the river
to the Pavilion of Lost Shoes.

Random, isolate, irrelevant finally,
shoes were scattered everywhere . . .
unless they just shoved them aside,
kicked them crazily across the room,
where would their shoes go? Besides

it was time they were out there
getting into real trouble . . . thugs,
patricidal maniacs on speed-skates
who narrowly jumped the open water
at the barricades, then disappeared

into the tangled, boreal forests
of the Black Lagoon. In those days
you could skate back there forever . . .
or you could limp back half frozen
and not be able to find your shoes.

I can still see them wincing along
to the bus stop, hobbling along
to the streetcar, their ankles broken
or looking somehow chained together . . .
prisoners for life, mere children.

ROBERTA AND WILBUR

First, we made them a gift
of toothpaste and some soap—
then Kathleen poured perfume
on Roberta's hair. We washed
Wilbur's face in the snow . . .

But they showed up anyway
day after day with their dry
peppery and uriniferous stink
without socks on, without hats
with pinworms, acne, dandruff . . .

Roberta, wall-eyed, smiling crazily
no matter what, and brother Wilbur
who stuttered, foamed and spit
and even exposed himself once
out of rage so pure, so impotent

a few stunned flakes of snow
fell stumbling down and melted
in my hair. A loose chain somewhere
kept clanking in the wind. A streetcar
passed out of hearing with a sigh . . .

And then we mobbed him. We chased
Roberta with his underwear, the gray
leprous flag of we who were spared
for no good reason, for nothing at all
the bottomless misery of the world.

STARSHIP LANDS
IN CORNFIELD!

—Headline, *Weekly World News*

A flying saucer has landed
upside down in a cornfield.

Except for being upside down
it looks scarcely damaged . . .

But one hears shouts in there—
throttled shrieks, a nickering

of pure, animal panic. Lights
or a kind of sentient glimmering

as in the eyes of beached whales
surface dimly in the portholes

and then sink back . . . *Nothing.*
No hope. Prepare yourselves.

Thus, one imagines, the captain
speaking to his crew. Meanwhile

across the highway, a school bus
pulls up and mutters to itself

beside a ditch of rusty ice . . .
It seems to be waiting on them:

the children from the starship.
Clumsy, alien, entirely at odds

with a lingering or fiery death
on this planet, they dawdle along

as if they had forever, hypnotized
by anything. Dogs, for instance.

Three dogs—mud-colored, snarling—
one with a glove in his mouth

charge furiously up and down
between some half-built houses—

delicate, ovicular dream houses
mired in a watery field littered

with corn stalks, squid shadows
the sudden darkness of the shark.

CREATIVE WRITING

One of my students
has written a story:

It's the end of the world
and an alien spaceship

is circling the planet
trying to make contact.

Hello? Anybody down there?
But it's just as they suspect.

After the atmosphere ignites—
nothing. Not a whimper. Even

our germs are dead. Now
they'll have to start over.

What a drag! Other planets
in the galaxy are doing fine

but you and I, the human race,
we just can't get it somehow.

Perhaps reptiles might work
or something underwater . . .

And so it goes for fifty pages—
fifty million years in fact,

one dimwit, evolutionary dud
after another—until finally

Homo Erectus! our old friend
back again. Talk about irony!

The best minds in the universe,
eon upon eon of experiment

and here we are, right back
where we started, doomed—

perfectly ignorant, oblivious
to art, language, metaphor . . .

yet hearing voices nonetheless,
the genius of creation itself

mumbling at us from a cloud.
So what can we do after all

but sweat blood, struggle,
learn to write it down—

never mind the spelling
the ribbon without ink—

the lords of the universe
are circling the planet

like moths around a desk lamp
and the whole dorm is asleep.

THE AFTERLIFE

Because all of it happens
at the speed of light

the soul naturally lingers
curious, appalled I think

near the impetuous corpse . . .
and as for all that whispering

from beyond the bright doorway
let them wait. I remember

when I was about ten or so
hitting my head on the ice

then waking up in the hospital
anonymous and all attention

beside a dead man. The man
had a hole in his neck . . .

I could identify the windpipe
but various other things

were in the dark. His hand
was close to my hand, one foot

hung off the cart . . . Someone
a name that would come to me

had simply dumped him there
slumped in his tangled IVs

like a let-go puppet. He knew
precisely who I was. The logic

of his bloodshot, puppet eye
was inescapable. The windows

too, were inescapable, black
the coldest dream of winter . . .

All the rivers were frozen —
trashcans wandered in the street

like tumbleweed. A child's name
in fact, might wander years

without a coat out there
without a hat or even socks

and I tried not to think of him
huddled under the overpass

or sleeping in doorways
too cold to speak.

BLUE TANGO

After stumbling around for months
like arthritic wooden puppets

unaccountably brain-damaged
and unable to count—failing

to fox-trot, failing to waltz
failing in the church basement

even to two-step correctly
it was decided we had danced

beyond all mere appearance
to some mystical new plateau

where henceforth we should learn
to tango. Our Dominican nuns

were adamant. The seventh grade
at the Assumption of Our Blessed

Virgin Mary School would tango!
The Saint Elizabeth's Sodality

with whom we shared the basement
on Wednesday afternoons agreed.

They loved that music; it helped
them sew. That year, I remember

they were busy sewing things
the nuns called "cancer pads."

And when the long, elliptical orbit
of our tango brought us twirling

close to the glimmering windows
the flimsy tables where they sewed

I'd hear the whispered variations
of a single, incessant conversation:

By the time they opened him up
repeated someone, *it was everywhere.*

Then off I'd go again, mincing
with my awkward too-tall partner

toward the gloomy furnace room.
Listening to those ladies talk

you'd think that suppurating cancers
had hit our parish like the plague.

Nor was there anything to do for it
but sewing cancer pads, communion

and learning, of course, to tango —
as if preparing for a long cruise

among the romantic blue islands
of the southern ocean. Some heaven

where even cabin boys could tango
and no one had to get up for work

at Packard's, Dodge Main, Cadillac . . .
where no one got pregnant, got cancer

lost their fingers in a punch press
or had even heard of Detroit, at all.

5

WHAT'S WRONG
WITH UFO'S?

> "I like happy endings sometimes
> don't you?"—Anon.

1

On the autumn shores
of Whitefish Lake

in his mother's cottage
trying to keep warm

a cold librarian, divorced
a member of Mensa

a watcher for UFO's
considers his situation:

perhaps he should place
an ad in some journal:

*sensual, intelligent man
53, desires someone . . .*

from another planet:
someone like his mother.

2

As a child, they'd drive
all night to Whitefish Lake

67

arriving for the loons
at daybreak, a whippoorwill

incessant, right through
breakfast: Time to swim.

Time to fish. Once
he got so excited

he had to run downhill
screaming: Wait! Wait

for me! Then he slammed
face first into a tree

and knocked himself out. Was
there something he should know?

3

You could have killed yourself
his mother said. He thinks

his ESP must date from then.
Yes . . . his photographic memory

recalls it perfectly: the wasp
the outboard motor . . . It seems

his spirit had temporarily
left his body and hovered

there, on the waspy ceiling
of the screened-in porch.

It was uncanny all right:
the motorboat had left

without him. His mother
was kissing someone else.

4

Who do you think you are?
his wife was always saying.

It got pretty confusing . . .
he was never quite sure.

But at night, sometimes,
just before sleep

he'd close his eyes
and see this wonderfully

luminous face. In the background
bright flags were fluttering.

It was him of course.
His astral body probably.

He began to see flying saucers too
and then his wife left him.

5

He despised self-pity
so when his mother died

he moved up here to the lake
and devoted himself entirely

to learning his full potential.
Aliens from another galaxy

however, were following him
to work. He had photographs.

Witnesses: old Mrs. Wanless
and her hunchbacked mother.

Lars, who ran the bait store
and could radiate light

from his fingertips. They
saw those flying saucers too.

6

Perhaps he was being considered
for some important mission.

It made good sense to him.
It began to fit and fit:

all he had to do was stay alive
and show them he was worthy.

Meanwhile, it had started to snow.
Tomorrow, the lake would freeze.

He'd been out of wood for a week
and had to burn scrap lumber

odd sticks of driftwood
and the driftwood lawn chairs.

Then he burned his mother's table
and all his wife's old books.

7

It was just about this time
he clairvoyantly perceived

the troubled mother ship
returning at light-speed

through the Crab Nebula.
There had been an accident

it seemed—a burned-out
crystal maybe in galactic

overdrive, a leak perhaps
in the antigravitation coil.

Anyway, he was almost frantic.
The mother ship was coming back!

He felt like a little kid.
He felt like screaming.

PART TWO

1

Knock, knock said the door.
He was afraid of the door . . .

He was afraid for his heart.
Then he heard this whimpering

like an animal of some kind—
a small bear or wolverine . . .

He was sure of it. In a book
he once loved best as a child

it wore a little red coat
like the one in the porchlight.

It was trying to stand up
in the backdoor porchlight . . .

"Please help me" said the bear
"I've just wrecked my car."

2

It took him a long time
before he finally got it:

a woman was bleeding to death
on his mother's porch. *Quick*

said the blood, *do something.*
But he could barely move . . .

His spirit had temporarily
left his body again. He

could even see it out there:
a kind of ectoplasmic snow

swirling up like plankton
through the frozen trees . . .

Meanwhile, she'd found the sink
and cleaned herself up a little.

3

"I could sure use a drink"
she whispered, lying wanly

on his mother's bed. Blood
was seeping through the towel

but he got her a drink anyway.
What was he supposed to do?

If his Volvo had a battery
if his spirit would stick around

he could drive her to Duluth . . .
Otherwise, there they were

drinking mother's scotch
and waiting for the police.

The policemen were amazed.
Her car had "virtually exploded."

4

He had to laugh at that one.
She was on her feet in no time

but he stayed sick for months.
He was anemic. His heart raced

and when she came to visit
an orderly unlocked the door . . .

Marcia taught first through four
at Spooner. But her nervous hands

her breasts, her perfect ears
made conversation difficult . . .

She came to see him often
because it was all her fault.

Because she was 48, a drunk
and he'd saved her after all.

5

"What's wrong with UFO's?"
said Marcia. She didn't care.

She said she'd like to see one.
They were on the ninth floor

looking down at Lake Superior.
Beyond the heaped-up inshore ice

a tiny, black insect of a boat
was pushing at a larger one.

"Dead in the water" he said.
It sounded final, definitive.

They were waiting for his things
then she was going to drive him

back down to his mother's place.
She'd been living there for weeks.

6

The place was certainly different.
Clean for one thing. And hot.

Marcia kept it in the 80s.
"That way," she said, "if we want

we can just wear underwear . . . "
She was vulgar, suffocating.

She crocheted little animals,
She said she loved him

but whenever they were drinking
she cried. She'd cry all day.

He was shouting in his sleep . . .
But what was it? Waking up

his mind was a white-capped field
of gray, exploded milkweed . . .

7

Time to fish said the lake
Time to swim said Marcia.

But all that summer into fall
his feckless, wayward spirit

glanced around like lights
glancing from a tiny mirror

or made a sound like water
pouring through the trees . . .

What was he supposed to do?
Move. Take a goddamn swim

said Marcia. She was sounding
even angrier than his mother . . .

walking toward him from the raft
naked, with a can of beer.

WHO'S THERE?

Someone at the window
rigid, afraid to move
her head half turned

as if she heard something—
voices, just now, back
inside the house somewhere . . .

Outside, the yellow trees
are flecked with robins
preparing their migrations

and in the done-for garden
where nothing grows so well
as hemlock now, or nightshade
or the sudden, deadly amanita

the fatalist rabbit
gives pause too—

a soft, peach light
lighting up the whole
cathedral of his ear.

Who's there?

No one. Another mouse perhaps.
Birds aflutter in the chimney . . .

Who's there?

Small leaves in a whirlwind
and the bright trees faltering
for a moment, like candles
in an upstairs window . . .

And so it is at middle age—
the spirit grows apprehensive
in the dark, autumnal house
of the body . . .

Turn on the TV for Christ's sake.
We can watch the news at least.

Or one can sit here listening . . .
the palest avatars of frost
forcing up the floorboards

whispering their benedictions
among the fat blue flies
dying on the windowsill.

THE BOTTOM LINE

I've lost my only pair of glasses;
without them, I'm practically blind

and so my cadaverous optometrist
signals me into his dim office.

"Have a seat," he says. He means
the chair with all the apparatus.

But he's pointing somewhere else —
as if I should sit on the floor

or maybe at his desk, gazing up
at all his marvelous diplomas.

"Well now, let's see," he says —
but when he turns, he bangs hard

into the filing cabinet . . . then
his hands move over the cabinet

to the wall, hunting for his charts.
"They're here someplace," he says.

Whereupon he reaches the window
and carefully pulls down the shade.

"Now tell me," he wants to know
"can you read the bottom line?"

He must be dreaming. I'm glad enough
to see the hand in front of my face

my poor wristwatch, glimmering now
like something deeply underwater . . .

"Just do the best you can," he yawns—
and then ensues an anguished snoring

the sounds of someone really drowning
a prolonged and horrible strangulation.

"Asphyxiation!" I shout. "Dead birds
in the chimney. Leaves. Loose mortar . . . "

But by this time, of course, the poor guy
is probably dead . . . And for all I know

his shy, receptionist wife is also dead.
Their dog is dead. Anything is possible

including a dollar fifty in small change
and the beat-up glasses of a whole universe

sitting dimly on a dead man's dresser—
all of it is possible. Even the bright

tiny, and altogether ridiculous moon
shining like a tear in each thick lens.

CAT'S PAW

The president is speaking
but I'm a long way off—

as far north apparently
as Labrador or Finland

some desperate latitude
where everything is wet

or frozen solid. A wet
black road, black trees

glittering with ice . . .
then a dead-still lake

a cottage leaking smoke.
Inside, the Muse herself—

dazed by too much television
lost in anchoritic gloom . . .

But now she's found at last.
It's spring! A cat's paw

ripples far, far out
across the lake. Then

the curtains move
and birdlike shadows

flutter in the mirror
where we undress . . .

Nevertheless, downstairs
all but forgotten

on the flickering tube
our uncanny president

turns suddenly passionate.
He wants to bomb something—

Libya, or maybe Finland . . .
It's hard to tell. Static

and other voices interfere.
It all sounds vaguely

like a bad war movie—
or maybe a motorcycle gang

getting stoned down there,
impatient for their turn.

In any case, the Muse
is not amused. She thinks

I ought to do something—
her poor heart beating

like some exquisite bird
the cat might catch

a hummingbird, a finch
a toy still fluttering.

HAMBURGER HEAVEN

A man orders a hamburger
but before he can eat it

he falls off his stool
foaming at the mouth . . .

What is it they tell you
to do with their tongue?

No one, not one customer
in all of Hamburger Heaven

has the foggiest notion.
So maybe the best thing

is to just move over—
give the guy some room.

But this guy is bleeding.
His face is turning blue.

He needs somebody strong
to force open his mouth.

He needs something to bite on
before he breaks his teeth.

His pants are wet. His head
keeps banging on the floor—

on the dumb-fuck cement
of Things-As-They-Are

until finally the loose
feckless white flag

of his Nike flies off
and it's over. Outside

in the slush somewhere
a Salvation Army Santa

rings a faint, faint bell—
but it tastes like blood.

His pants are wet. Then
a blond, ethereal waitress

hands him a shoe—enormous
in his slow comprehension

and heavy as death. Now
he can try to remember

why it was he was born
and the reason for hell

not to mention his name
or the secret of tongues

or what it was exactly
he'd specifically ordered.

ATLANTIS

Stopped for a stoplight
he looks down from an overpass
into a street of little stores—

a party store, cut-rate furniture . . .
stores with boards on the windows
and doorways filled with trash.

Little whirlwinds of cellophane,
leaves and paper cups start up—
then a flurry of plastic bags

like jellyfish, go swimming by . . .
as if he were looking down
from inside a submarine perhaps

at some ancient, weed-dense city—
some lost and blear Atlantis
stirring eerily to life again

under the piss-colored light
of his sodium lamps. Old stoves
toilets, some burned-up cars . . .

piles and troves like these
fill whole backyards down there—
bedsprings, washing machines

a bathtub full of bricks . . .
as if, in the last days,
collecting junk like this

became a form of prayer. Then
the light turns green again
and he's back on the interstate

listening to the news. Something
about "Humanitarian Aid." Contras
Russian tanks in Nicaragua . . .

but his mind is somewhere else.
In the cold, atavistic muck
just behind him in the dark

something big has been disturbed—
a giant eel, a rope of mucous
the steady coiling and uncoiling

of a wormlike, blind indifference
that feeds upon the drowned
the poor too poor to withstand

the first, least wave of unemployment
the smallest kind of war
children buried in the rubble

dragonflies, like gunships,
hovering over some putrescence
on the weedy shore.